Play Ball
HOME RUNS FOR LIFE

Robert W. Lowe Jr.

PLAY BALL · HOME RUNS FOR LIFE

Great American Opportunities Inc./FRP

President: Thomas F. McDow III
Managing Editor: Mary Cummings
Project Manager: Judy Jackson
Creative and Product Manager: Karen Bird
Editors: Linda Bennie, Linda Jones, Carolyn King
Art Director: Steve Newman
Production Designer: Bill Kersey
Production: Mark Sloan
Manufacturing Assistant: George McAllister

Published by
Great American Opportunities Inc.
P.O. Box 305142
Nashville, Tennessee 37230

Library of Congress Cataloging-in-Publication Data
Lowe, Robert W., 1968-
Play ball: home runs for life/Robert W. Lowe, Jr.
p. cm.
ISBN 0-87197-451-7
1. Success—Psychological aspects.   I. Title.
BF637.S8L7 1996
158—dc21   96-44095

Dedication

This book is dedicated to the Green Hills/Lipscomb
"Cubs" and, of course, our faithful
scorekeeper, my wife, Stephanie.

This book is not authorized by any of the youth
baseball leagues, but it endorses all of them.

Introduction

As a twenty-something member of Generation X, I was ordained
an adult by receiving my college diploma. I was struggling to find
success in all areas of my life. In spite of having read a
bookstore-full of self-help books, I found many of the principles
I now live by in the most common of childhood experiences.
As a young player, I didn't realize what I was learning as
I lived from corn dog to the free post-game Coke®.

But fifteen years later, as I wandered onto a local Little League field as an assistant coach, I became aware of the education I had received many years before. It was during this one amazing season, filled with heart-stopping wins and knee-weakening losses, that I realized the simple life lessons that I had learned from America's last perfect game—youth league baseball.

Robert W. Lowe .Jr.

Rarely do you find a great first-pitch hitter.

Being prepared will distinguish you from the others.

Your mother and your coach expect you to get your uniform dirty.

Success is generally the result of hard work and commitment. Without these, there is little anyone can do to help you.

The visiting team always bats first.

Let your guests go first.

The home team always gets to bat last.

There is no place like home.

Everyone gets to play.

Treat everyone equally and with respect.

When it rains, we don't play.

Sometimes, no matter how much you desire and work toward a goal, you cannot achieve it immediately. Accept this truth; remain focused and be patient.

When you're pitching, the umpire will miss a call or two or three.

There will be times when you don't get the credit you deserve.

Strike!
—William Shakespeare

When you're batting, the umpire will miss a call or two or three.

Decisions will be made that, for whatever reason,
you just have to accept.

When the umpire blows a call, your coach will generally let it be known.

Good parents, coaches, or friends will watch out for the interests of their child, player, or friend.

When the game gets close, the coach will play the best players.

The most capable people will get the most responsibility.

The best player for the position doesn't always get to play that position.

Unfortunately, responsibilities are not always assigned to the individual best suited for the job.

When batting, there is a chance that you'll get hit by the pitch and that it's going to hurt.

Throughout life, disappointments are going to hurt.
But time and faith heal all wounds.

When hit by a pitch, take first base.

When treated unfairly, seek retribution.

When you get hit fielding a ground ball, shake it off.

Roll with the punches.

A good outfielder always hits the cut-off man.

Working as a team makes you and your co-workers
stronger and more efficient and creates
fewer chances for mistakes.

In youth leagues there are no lead-offs.

When learning a new skill, keep it simple.
The bells and whistles are just complexities
that have little to do with the heart of the skill.

If your pitcher can't throw strikes, it's going to be a long day.

If your proposal doesn't meet your clients'
or customers' needs, it won't be accepted.

All parents want their child to play.

Your parents want the best for you.
For this we should all be grateful.

It often seems as though one player's error lost the game.

On a team, one individual is rarely the sole cause of a failure. More often, a majority of the team could have changed the outcome but did not.

Training is everything. The peach was once a bitter
almond; cauliflower is nothing but cabbage
with a college education.
        —**Mark Twain**

The best teams practice, practice, practice.

Keep learning. Through education you can achieve anything you desire.

It takes time to break in a new glove.

New ideas and technologies will not be automatically accepted. Through perseverance and educating others, you can encourage acceptance of your ideas.

Every batter must wear a helmet.

Every day we risk injury. Take precautions.

A runner must stay within the base path or be called out.

If you break the law or violate ethical behavior, you will eventually lose.

A batter must hit the ball within the field of play or it's not a hit.

To achieve success, you must know the rules and regulations governing your occupation and abide by them.

Three strikes and you're out.

Everyone deserves forgiveness.
However, if you're unwilling to learn from your
mistakes, you're unlikely to succeed.

The pitcher gets four balls and the batter only three strikes.

If you're trying to take market share away from an existing company, you'll be expected to do more to earn the business.

Take your hat off for the national anthem.

There are freedoms for which we should all be eternally grateful.

No tobacco.

Take care of your mind, body, and soul.

The players are in charge of picking up the equipment.

Either accept this aspect and pull your weight,
or try your own business.

Warm up before the game.

Preparation is a key to success.

Not everyone makes the all-star team.

The most skilled individuals will generally
be given the most opportunity.

Don't always swing for the fence.

Break your goals down into manageable steps.

A bunt counts as a hit in the score book.

Don't underestimate the significance of a small contribution to the project.

A Hall of Fame hitter will be called out two out of three times at bat.

You will not succeed at every venture in your life. Don't confuse failure with lack of effort or preparation. It is much better to strive for your goals and fall short than not to try at all.

A sacrifice bunt or fly can help your team win.

The people behind the scenes deserve as much recognition as those in the limelight. Be appreciative of those individuals in your life who support and encourage you.

Errors happen.

People make mistakes. The individual committing the
mistakes should acknowledge personal responsibility;
co-workers should lend encouragement to regain
focus toward the goal.

A **double play** is a beautiful thing.

From time to time, you will have the opportunity
to capitalize on a given situation. If you are well
prepared and remain focused, you will achieve
success and make it look easy.

One inning can change an entire game.

Don't allow failures or negative individuals to dissuade you from achieving your goals. Each day offers new challenges and opportunities. Meet your challenges head on, and embrace your opportunities.

Sometimes cleaning off home plate can help the umpire.

It is possible to work so intensely toward a goal that you lose sight of the significant things in life. Write down the people and things that you are most grateful for, and read this list daily.

Pitchers are limited to a specific number of innings per game and per week.

Take time to relax and rejuvenate your mind and body.
This is not only healthy, but will allow you to perform better.

Parents want to help because they remember this wonderful game fondly.

Watch and listen to those who are willing to help and teach you. You'll learn a great deal, and it's a terrific opportunity to develop new friendships.

Physical errors cannot be avoided. Mental errors can be.

Everyone makes mistakes from time to time;
however, mistakes from lack of planning,
preparation, or mental focus can be avoided.

Each team has twelve players.

People go on vacation. A good company will anticipate and encourage this.

Your best player will oftentimes miss the biggest game of the season.

A business too dependent on one individual is risking failure.

A seven- to ten-run inning is not unusual and will occur when you're least expecting it.

Never assume you have reached your goal until you have, and don't underestimate others' ability to overcome setbacks and challenge you again.

A team will practice wherever there is an open field.

Don't be as concerned about aesthetics as about hard work toward your goal.

The person most likely to get kicked out of the ball park is an adult.

Sometimes, as we grow older, we fail to recognize a game is just a game.

Any player late for practice is going to run laps.

Being on time is a sign of responsibility and respect.

Any player missing practice won't get to play in the next game.

Every action, whether intentional or unintentional, has an outcome for which each individual should be held personally responsible.

Once a player has worked off the penalty, the coach and other players forget about it.

If individuals are not held accountable for their actions, co-workers resent the inequality in their workplace.

The umpire behind the plate also wears protective gear.

If you find yourself drawn into someone else's argument, be extremely careful not to get hurt yourself.

There is no designated hitter.

Include those individuals who don't expect to be included.

Players are not allowed to go swimming the day of a game.

All goals in life require some aspect of personal sacrifice.

Most teams have sponsors.

Most start-up ventures require that you find others willing to support you, financially or otherwise.

The season will *go better* if the coaches start off with a parents' meeting.

It is important in any venture to understand what outside factors, both positive and negative, could affect your progress. Identifying these factors and respecting their influence may help you maximize the positive influences and minimize the negative ones.

Any player hit by a pitch during a game gets a pack of "Screaming Sours" candies at the next practice.

Take a negative that occurs during the regular performance of your job and associate a fun or positive event with it. Then you and your co-workers won't always be avoiding that possibility.

The inning is generally influenced by whether the lead-off batter (commonly referred to as the leading lady) gets on base.

On most projects, beginning on a positive note will help to get the momentum going in your favor.

It's the coach's job to see that everyone is loose and not playing under too much pressure.

Strive to help your co-workers lower the tension while remaining focused during a stressful project or negotiation. Everyone will feel better, and the chances of success will be increased.

Right field is often the site of the most exciting plays.

Anticipate that the least skilled member of
your team may be challenged directly.

Before the ball is pitched, think about what you are going to do if the ball is hit to you.

Be prepared; you never know when you'll get your chance.

Back up every throw.

Be there for your friends when they need you. You may
be able to minimize their injuries from their own
mistakes or someone else's.

Follow through when you throw the ball.

Never leave a job unfinished.

A good pitcher throws a first-pitch strike to get ahead of the hitter.

First impressions count. Be on time, and be prepared.

Keep your eye on the ball.

Remain focused on your goals.

A good batter makes the pitcher throw a strike.

In all negotiations, wait for a good offer before accepting.
All too often, it won't be the first one.

Don't swing at balls pitched over your head.

Don't be distracted by grandiose dreams. Set realistic goals, achieve them, and then set new goals.

And so I shall catch the fly.
—William Shakespeare

Use two hands when catching a fly ball.

Most errors occur when you get complacent or show off.

Never make the third out at third base.

When you're close to reaching your goal, remain focused. Don't risk failure to gain something that won't help you achieve your goal.

If the play at the plate is going to be close, slide!

Find out what it will take to achieve
your goals and go for it!

It ain't over till it's over.
—Yogi Berra

A good batter always runs out all fly balls.

Exhaust all possibilities. Oftentimes answers to problems present themselves to those who see a project to its conclusion, regardless of the apparent outcome.

The runners will advance on wild pitches that get past the catcher.

Do not be naive. When you make a mistake, many people will take advantage of the situation if they can.

When you hit a home run, you get to take your time and jog around the bases.

Following success, take time to enjoy your accomplishment and to understand how you achieved your goal.

When caught in a rundown, force a throw, then run as hard as you can toward the base away from the player with the ball.

When you make a mistake, immediately recognize and admit it. Try to correct it as soon as possible.

When running the bases, check the runner in front of you before advancing.

If a project requires others to accomplish a task first, be sure they are aware of your expectations and respect their judgment. No one will benefit if you achieve your goal only to have the project fail.

Good pitchers throw inside pitches.

Expect your competition to challenge
your weaknesses, avoid your strengths, and
compete to the best of their ability.

Good fielders keep their body in front of the ball.

Anticipate mistakes and be prepared
to minimize their negative impact.

When you're on deck, swing a weighted bat or a bat with a donut on it.

Train harder and prepare more than the actual event should require.

Aggressive base running is rewarded if you're safe.

Every action we take has a commensurate outcome or risk. Be mindful of the potential consequences of your actions, and be willing to accept personal responsibility for both positive and negative results.

If you get caught stealing, you're out!

If you get caught stealing, you're out!

Always call a fly ball.

Let those around you know what you expect of them, and ask them what they expect of you. Clearly defining everyone's responsibilities up front not only avoids problems, it will oftentimes create efficiencies.

Three balls and one strike is a hitter's pitch.

There are situations in every occupation in which the odds of success are greatly increased. Know when this advantage occurs in your profession, and be prepared to seize the opportunity.

With a count of 0-and-2, good pitchers rarely throw a pitch that the batter can hit.

Regardless of how easily it appears you're reaching your goals, you must remain focused to maintain the advantage you've gained.

When the count is 3-and-0, the batter will take the pitch, forcing the pitcher to throw a strike or give up a walk.

When the odds are against you, don't expect help. Keep your composure, and give it your best effort.

When the count is 3-and-0, the umpire will generally call a close pitch a strike.

In a meeting, everyone wants to reach the objectives of the meeting, not get bogged down in details or errors created by one person.

On a shallow fly ball to the outfield, the outfielder should call off the infielder when she believes she can catch the ball.

If two team members are capable of completing a task, the individual who can do the job with the least amount of risk to the overall goal should speak up and take responsibility to eliminate confusion.

Players in the field should chatter to support their pitcher.

Verbally supporting a co-worker gives that person encouragement and intensifies your concentration on the goal at hand.

In order to win, all players must be ready to make the play when they get their chance.

Business is a team endeavor dependent on individual accomplishments.

A good coach pays attention to the bat size each player selects. Players sometimes overestimate their physical abilities.

Optimism is an essential characteristic in achieving your goals. However, optimism should never blind you to the realities.

When pitching, focus on the batter, not on the base runners.

Once you learn your profession, success is in large part dependent upon your perception of yourself and your ability to maintain the focus on your goals.

When fielding a ground ball, stay down and always keep your glove on the ground.

Doing the things that are hard or uncomfortable, such as working longer hours, getting up earlier, and studying more, can help you succeed.

The batter on deck is responsible for making sure the equipment is inside the dugout.

Clearly defining responsibilities eliminates confusion.

Sticks in a bundle are unbreakable.
—East African saying

Late in the game, when you're losing but are within striking distance of taking the lead, put on your "rally cap." (Rally caps are simply caps turned inside out.)

When a deadline is near, a great deal of momentum can be gained through acts of solidarity. No matter how simple the act, the fact that everyone is saying, "We're in this together," can be incredibly empowering.

Remember to tag up on a fly ball.

Positive actions can usually be taken in response to negative events. However, you can lose even more ground by allowing yourself to agonize over prior mistakes and miss the opportunity to capitalize on these proactive moves.

With two outs and a full count, the base runners should be running on the pitch.

Recognize crucial moments and give it everything you've got to move ahead.

The runners on base should watch the first- and third-base coaches instead of where the ball was hit.

When you are involved in an intense negotiation or competition, turn to a knowledgeable person you trust for advice. Being a step away from the action may help this person give you a perspective you otherwise wouldn't be aware of.

When you are running the bases, make sure you tag every base.

Too often, when we are moving quickly toward our goals, we become careless and fail to attend to the small details. It is precisely when everything seems to be going well that you need to intensify your focus on the details that helped you get to that point.

When you are at bat, you get an unlimited number of foul tips.

As long as you continue to put forth honest effort and are close to reaching your goals, you can expect to continue to get new opportunities.

When there is a pop fly in the infield, the catcher should shout out whose ball it is.

The person with the best vantage point should make the decisions.

It is a happy talent to know how to play.
—**Emerson**
<u>Journals</u>, 1834

When you hit a home run, you get to keep the ball.

Keep a little reminder of every success. When times are not so great or you've had a setback, go through these mementos. This reinforcement will help your resolve to continue toward your goals.

Never watch a third-strike pitch. Always go down swinging.

When you are facing a setback or even a failure,
don't give up. Bear down and give it your best.

To turn a double play, the shortstop or second baseman must make sure to first catch the ball.

When you are making a presentation or proposal, be sure that the basis for your opinion is clearly defined and understood.

If a team is winning by ten runs or more after the fourth inning, the game is over (this is known as the mercy rule).

When you achieve your goal, do everything you can to see that those who didn't triumph are not humiliated.

When it's late in the game, one run will beat you, and there is a runner on third with fewer than two outs, pull your outfielders in far enough that they have a chance to throw out the runner at home.

When your company is young or near failure, winning a large contract won't help if you can't fulfill your end of the agreement.

When you go up to bat, make sure you take your cuts.

The only way to reach your goals is to take your best shot and risk failure.

From time to time, a ball is hit hard directly to the one player on the field that everyone thinks can't make the play.
Somehow he *does*.

Don't let anyone tell you that you can't reach your goals. Faith, determination, and hard work can lead to your success and others' surprise.

Once the lineup is made and the game has begun, a coach can do very little to put better batters up in different situations.

Everyone deserves the chance to contribute to the team as well as to their own goals.

When you drop the ball you're fielding, pick it up with your bare hand instead of your gloved hand.

When you make a mistake, don't make excuses or get fancy to cover it up. Admit your mistake and act quickly to correct it in the most efficient manner.

A good catcher always gives the pitcher a good target with the mitt.

Give your employees or co-workers a clear understanding of what is expected of them.

When the ball is hit in the air, an outfielder's first step should be backwards.

When considering how to handle a problem, it generally helps to step away and view it in a different light so that you can attack it directly with the best solution.

A good coach is always trying to get runners in scoring position.

When building a business, it is important to meet with as many prospective clients or customers as possible.

Good players do not try to throw out a runner who is almost to the base.

Recognizing that you can't prevent a mistake from occurring can help you not to compound its negative effect.

When the catcher drops a third-strike pitch, the batter has the opportunity to beat out the throw to first.

Knowing all aspects of your business will give you the ability to turn some errors into successes.

The players on the bench
seldom know how many outs
there are—and often
don't even know the score.

Staying involved in the day-to-day operations of a business
makes it easier to maintain an accurate perspective.

Win or lose, there will be a team meeting after the game.

Each day, take time to appreciate the wonderful blessings in your life.

In our play we reveal what kind of people we are.
—**Ovid**
<u>The Art of Love</u> (C.A.D. 8)

Shake hands after the game... win or lose.

Acknowledging a good effort in either victory or defeat is not only good sportsmanship but will remind us that this event is only a game, only a business decision, etc. Tomorrow is a new day.

After the game, win or lose, be sure to get your free Coke®.

Let kids be kids.

At the end of the season, there is always a team picnic.

Because team morale is crucial, reward hard work and celebrate improvements regardless of whether the project was successful. There will be another opportunity.

From time to time, you will lose the "Big Game."

Failure is common. Resilience and persistence thereafter are the precursors to success.

Kids are sometimes late for practice and games because their parents didn't get them there on time.

Although family events and problems can affect your productivity, you must accept the ultimate responsibility for maintaining and/or regaining your focus.

Once the game is over, the king and the pawn go
back into the same box.
—Italian saying

After the game, all the kids run off and play together.

Business is business, and, as long as everyone plays hard and ethically, it should not detract from friendships.

When we win the "Big Game," we're going for pizza (and the coach is buying).

Celebrate successes! And, if you're the boss, reward your co-workers.